PLANTING LIGHT

ALSO BY ANNE BORN

Salcombe Shipyards
(Cock Robin Press 1978;
Dartington Poetry Press, reprint, 1978)
Airy Lines
(Hub Publications 1978)
Changing Views
(Midday Publications 1979)
Lighting Effects
(Headland Publications 1987)
Figures for Landscape
(Headland Publications 1990)
Poems of Landscape (with Keith Spencer)
(Spacex Gallery 1990)
Drake
(Westwords Publications 1993)
Seeing through
(Blue Button Press 1994)
Slant as an open door
(Odyssey Poets 1994)
Histories (with Alex Smith)
(Salzburg 1998)

Thank you for the music!

PLANTING LIGHT

Anne Born

Anne Born

HEADLAND

First published in 1999
by
HEADLAND PUBLICATIONS
38 York Avenue, West Kirby,
Wirral, Merseyside. L48 3JF

A full CIP record for this book is available
from the British Library

ISBN 1 902096 58 4

supported by north west arts board

HEADLAND acknowledges the financial assistance of North West Arts Board

Printed in Great Britain by
Gee & Son Ltd, Denbigh.

Acknowledgements

Thanks to these magazines:
Acumen, Iron, Odyssey, Litup!, Oasis, Other Poetry, Scratch, Seam, Second Shift, Smith's Knoll, The Bound Spiral, Tremblestone, Rustic Rub, Interactions.

And these anthologies:
An idea of Bosnia (Autumn House), *Klaonica, poems for Bosnia* (Bloodaxe), *Exposing the Negatives* (The Old School Press), *The West in her Eye* (Pyramid Press), *Jersey Eisteddfod Competition Anthology*. Also to the Royal Devon & Exeter Hospital poetry competition/display, *Ways With Words Competition Anthology 1998.*

Special thanks to the editors of *Rustic Rub* (Jay Wodman) who published the sequence *A break in time*, and the editor of *The Transactions of The Devonshire Association* (Dr Tom Greeves), who published the sequence *Hillson* (1994 & 1995 resp.)

Cover design by Simon Drew.

CONTENTS

Meanings

Hillson

A break in time

Occurrences

WOMAN AND CHICKENS

There was a sense of metal in the light
when she woke at dark's end that morning
remembering a dream about three chickens
escaped and waiting, free with an air
of contemplation at a traffic junction.
They took no notice of any man or woman

until they took a few steps towards one woman
who wondered what they thought of the light
pouring its golden grain on the traffic junction
in an extraordinary deluge that common morning.
Mineral or metal, cloudless light and air
turned them into eagles, those chickens.

She, who had never thought them dumb, chickens,
realised their heads held bird, as hers, woman
breathing and living in the challenge of air
in high room or wooden shed, in light
or shadow, recurrent as morning
waiting or decided at a junction.

For it's never straightforward, any junction
holds a choice of decision, for chickens
as well as women. On any morning
they must face acceptance or refusal, woman
and bird, to lock doors upon the light
or walk through into the open air:

chickens to scratch away at thick air
and take the amazing chance, fly to the junction,
jump into the stream against the light
accept the metal blow, not neckwrung chickens
without cluck, just as the woman
decides to walk free every morning.

Not in a pen, but a good morning
when she will sling her hat into the air
and see coming towards her another woman
busy attending to her particular junction.
She'll decide to greet the best of plucky chickens
their cool yellow feet, their sweet feather light.

Not many mornings do you see at the junction
bright in the air a trio of chickens
meeting a woman at first light.

SEAL TO WOMAN
WOMAN TO SEAL

A day blurred with green and grey,
fields swilled and soused with rain
flowing down to where
sky and sea weld in one
and no boundaries hold, no edges.

A call comes out of the smir,
a child, lost on the shore?
and again it comes, there, there,
Whoo, Whooo, downfalling
in a tone filled with loss.

Now I know what a seal knows,
lithe and light in the flow
that gives and takes, lifts and sinks,
sleeks what's sleek, invites
the dive and rise. But space
and depths part one from other,
muscle in on currents and tides,
brute strength of waters
drowns the grace of blood.

On Rousay's shore stones set
by hands two thousand years ago
stand firm against time's tides,
their origins more violent
than skin and flesh, their shelter
now the freehold of gull and vole.

Their atoms hold the history
of those foregone lives,
over transitions of seal to woman,
woman to seal. Both voice
sea sorrow, both echo
the functions of bone and stone.

RED WINE PANTOUM

Red wine is the blood of the sun
bled from vined veins of grapes
those bubbles of the flesh that come
like little worlds perfect shapes.

Bled from vined veins of grapes
decanted into a cask of wood
little worlds perfect shapes
liquefied for joy and good.

Decanted into a cask of wood
and left to sleep away from air
liquefied for joy and good
waiting for a foot on the stair.

Left to sleep away from air
until awake in a hand-cut glass
waiting for a foot on the stair
to let the sunlight in at last.

Awake in a hand-cut glass
raised high to start the singing
to let the sunlight in at last
lift hearts and send them soaring.

Raised high to start the singing
those bubbles of the flesh that come
to lift hearts and send them soaring.
Red wine is the blood of the sun.

RUNNING ON WATER

Treading her home ground waves
running on water before the wind
that fills her sails with speed
ignoring the depth beneath.
As a plane strides over air
unconscious of height
its wide and wind-cuffed slopes
she's effortless on a calm evening
sun westering
no falling through but landfall
over the last lap of horizon
at the estuary gate
A full tide brings her home
and the anchor splashes and drops
to bed
So we lock the front door again
peel the safety of a banana
have a coffee, bath and bed:
our night ship to sail us
running over oceans and dreams,
spars, skulls on the ground floor,
whatever waits before
the next tide of light.

SEAFEASTING

My clothes trail down the beach
as stepping stones to the depths
I'm in for now. Water, oh, my lover,
here I am to meet your high tide.

You seem cool but your strength
rocks me, holds me, covers me,
and what an appetite you give -
I dive deep for a handful of oysters,

thumbfinger flick them open
What ocean bouquet,
what exquisite slither,
salted with sea, peppered with sunspots.

I drink air champagne, chew seaweed bread,
dive again and come up with more.
We mingle our juices, sea and I,
know each other's ebb and flow.

I suck on a sand eel to tickle my tongue
as you lap around each crease and orifice,
smooth away tensions, whisper
sweet storms into my ear.

How you always draw me to come
in with your tides and depths and muscle,
your dangers. Oh my challenger,
how do I pit my passion against you?

FOXY

Suddenly
Out on the cliffs
she faced me: a vixen
with a pally intimate grin
that let me in on secrets
she seemed willing to pass on.
My clothes grew into skin
my feet were deft as hers.
She turned then, self-assured
went back into her life.
The place where she had been
emptied of her
except for a whiff of wildness
she'd shown me could somewhere be mine.

BLOWING HOUSE

The Glaze Brook's glides and falls
are corralled by granite-block walls
older than words. A pelt of moss
uniforms felspar, mica and quartz.

In turn high trees keep the walls in check:
their roots are arms that lie along the shoulders
of stones that can't shrug off.
They're above ground, not excavators
digging for rich metal underground.

Tinners' mould-stones gape for molten ore
under a roof of sky where an oaktree
grows atop a wall brought to its knees
that once housed men gripped by stone
streamed and smelted for the glitter of tin.

The stream's muscles ripple,
meet to pattern a constant fan of arcs,
a quiver of nerves on the surface, that huddles
to a sleek spout pouring out and down.

Grass gentles the ground. Tiny savages,
midges dervishly attack, dusk furies,
strong as rock in single-minded aim,
innumerable survivors where the old men's
flesh and bones are the breath of winds.

DRINKING COINTREAU WITH A DUTCHMAN, A DUTCHWOMAN AND A SWISS BY A PEAT FIRE IN COUNTY CLARE

We've had Irish seafood and Australian wine
with a westerly sizzling through window cracks
airily caressing our backs.
Now we sit drinking Dutch duty-free

near the wave-bashed coast of County Clare.
In the dark high up on the hill
ruined castle walls echo still
with battle-yells and higher

the wild pale rockscape of the Burren,
limestone terraces step by giant step,
clints and grikes gape to snap your ankles
and only owls and ravens croak and mourn

but in the grass at the heel of the rocks
spring gentians shine with astounding blue
and mountain avens open white, true
to a land surviving perhaps.

Down the road once lived a Nazi
in a house shuttered and barred
with dark hedge and electric fence, shaded
and tended by a wife he gauleitered

until he died. Then she roused to dance
and took up passion with a fine young man
who played the fiddle and sang, while they ran
down all the bumpy roads in Clare and Galway.

'It's time to start afresh,' says our host
at *The Admiral's Rest*, he hangs up his compass
and shows us flowers and rocks and how to pass
time and stop the blood of centuries.

So we sit and drink and laugh and talk
old friends of just an hour or two
on top of the world we're moving through
hoping old battered Europe's born anew.

IN ARBIN STREET, OSLO

Hard stairs curve up to the door
Inside, high ceilings, dark walls.
The study first, so visitors
don't intrude further. In the hall,
Ibsen can deal with timewasters:
'As long as you keep me talking
I can't write.' His desk looks out
to street and park. On one side:
the couch Susannah won't let him fall asleep on
and spoil his night's rest. On the other:
Strindberg's portrait. That presence
keeps his rival up to scratch, Ibsen
enjoys knowing he can work
when Strindberg can't. Between speeches
Ibsen studies 'the terrain of the face'
and feels happier, his round cheeks, thin lips,
that after all can smile, weathered
but not into the tortured crags of the Swede.

Through connecting doors, named rooms:
Red, Brown and Blue.
But dark enough to be a sombre stage
for these last years. Worn lino keeps the cold in.
(Susannah keeps all the windows tightly closed,
you need to hold your breath on going in).

And now the ritual walk to the café
and his cognac and strong ale is too far.
His world contracts to study, then to bedroom
and its balcony where people stand
on Karl Johan Street to gaze
upward at their own divinity.

The final week, and words are drowned
as the river nears the sea. He wants it.
The nurse says he's improved, he rears
to say 'Tvertimot.' She's wrong like so many
witless people who haven't understood him.
'On the contrary,' there's no holding him this time.
The curtain drops. Fin.

When Susannah nerves herself to come,
short hurting steps accented by stick-tap,
his face is smooth and beautiful.

LIVING IMAGES AT THE ACROPOLIS

My eyes are uppercut with light
as I climb steps shone by ages
or stop for breath in gifts of shade,
look down on Athens' wide spread
over the plains' soil-breadrock.

Columns and architraves carved from the hills
seem stone of the sun, dare dazzle it,
worked to such a pitch of strength
that two thousand years are minutes
and each life's time a second's flash.

I've travelled to tread Athena's stones
in what seemed an ordinary morning
walking through muscle-knotted olives
where cicadas revved perpetual motors
as flea-scratching dogs lolled in the hot wind.

To dogs we're just leglacking fools
wasting energy, scuffing up dust.
It's the golden stone lasts, not lads or girls.
But I stand time-travelling to gaze
and hear tongues wag in every tongue.

'You're on your own, shall I take your picture?'
I switch back to now, but I don't want
to be taken and shot out of my dream
of astonishment at a famous name
suddenly met with larger than my life.

Later I'll not want to see me
not even the pictures that *I* take
but the genius loci blazing gold
and its huge goddess as she stood
in the form created by a sculptor

close to beginnings, feeling the clout
of her wisdom, close to craft and light.
She stays on here, stays on now
among the crowds, in a child's profile,
an arched foot, as dogs bite fleas, cicadas sing.

FROM THE LOST PROPERTY LIST

Not paper dolls to call their own,
'the dolls that other fellas couldn't steal.'
no, blow-up ones, blubbers for loners
called early by mobile phones
who left seven dollies deflating.

In the white hotel morning, prone
and cast down on cold carpets
they didn't call up ardour.
Even with no word of parting
wept no tears of misery.

Seven men walked out still lonely,
melted into pin figures in airport,
city, station, their dolldreams'
breath turned to cold air,
eyes open shiny with blank stares.

Silence shrouds all abandoned ones
condemned to lost property's black bags,
cast offs of lives that seem to know
nothing best or something best not said.
Dreams fade, gather dust under beds.

HARUSPEX

She holds it in both hands
and feels its heat,
ripped from the still-supple
body of the sacrifice,
exactly matching hers.

Recalls how it divides
into sections for various signs,
and then divines. The god of life
enters both beast's liver
and human brain, engenders
words for her to soothsay.

Studying the redbrown gut
she sees through sick men's hearts,
ailing body parts, fevers.
Or descries a king's ambition,
outcomes of wars plotted in the dark,
the lie of enemy land.

Sees, shaking, the fall of walls,
ruin of terracotta busts, friezes,
the leap of a horse at speed, broken,
rooftiles smashed and buried.
Wishes an end to her art,
the cleansing liver back in its body.

THE TURLOUGH AT COOLE

Water sinks into the ground
as skies fade at evening
drops into a sudden well
down into limestone courses
depths away from light
to well up miles away.

The lake that stretches wide
for Yeats's 59 swans
leaves them a high and dry summer
as the bed offers pasture to cattle
and a soft resting place.

The fluency of water
its presence here and now
before absence, and then under
what seems firm ground
riddled with pothole and passage.

Yet flows on unseen unheard
in a confluence of veins
then reappears when summer's
white seas and dusty answers
fall back before the rains
veil and refill the ground.

Turlough: (Irish), pond or lake that dries in summer.

Western Australia

GOING DOWN UNDER

Go to the big land, they told us
the old ones too weak for the water.
Go. So we left our homegrounds
and took on the ocean. No sound now
of hammering wood into boat

from a tree gutted of rings
chopped from its root-anchor
dead and quiet on the earth
ready for hands and axes
coming to life on water.

I was at the foremost point
of that boat, a lookout for changes
in waves or weather. The ocean
mumbled under dry feet.
Fish. Gangs of dolphins. Shark's fin.

The sun dried everything. Wood,
hands, hair, eyes, food and water.
The salt sea hurt. The dark
wasn't dark enough. Stars were thorns.
We sang in voices brittle as twigs.

They gave me the last of the water,
but soon my mouth was sapless
I looked out still, heard sound
far off like wind in the trees.
A bird came, a white seabird.

Another. An arrow found crimson
whiteness fell and they turned
the boat, caught the winged fish
and tore it, ate feathers and flesh.
Gave me a piece but I could not.

Then we saw red land nearing,
pulling us in to white teeth
eating a beach. Waves rose
bucking like cattle. The boat
threw all of us into the sea.

I see our homeplace, my mother.
Water her arms, she pulls me.
I am water, I've left air, I'm heavy
hurting and filled with the dark
as I fall the deep way to dreamtime.

'LISTEN TO THE LAND'
Australian Aborigine

Its breath loud in midday wind
faint in sleep through a desert night
or shallow in terrible midmorning sun.

Its skin cracking under your feet
or trickling grains on the dunes
or rolling boulders down heights.

Its intestinal waters and sweating rivers
that lap and flow through dreams,
and its parched throat that gasps.

The clack of its bones that fall apart
the crack of its forests in fire
the soft opening of uncountable flowers.

Its loud secret voices like birds
that sing, hoot, wail, and laugh.
Train your ears to pick out sounds
that are your own language,
the words you knew down ages,
the significance of distances.

AFTER THE STIRLING RANGES, THE KARRI FORESTS, WA

James Stirling stood here
two centuries back
looking over the breasted hills
wondering

how his boots could tread the bush
into submission,
thorn, snake, iron-trunked grass-tree,
deadly spider.

Haloed with insistent flies
and merciless sun
fell on his knees before
the gold blaze of a Christmas tree

Christ never knew
and pushed on down
into the incomprehensible shade
of tall straight karri trees.

RED EARTH

Forget green except as a fringe benefit
in coastal forests or darkened by heat
Red is the world here, and ochre.
Red as blood under black skin, the beat

of sun early and late. Earth
that's ground, carpet, habitat,
the hearth fire lives on, they know
its dust their mattress and state.

In its warm welcome the child's legs
are buried, playthings unlimited
surround her, she takes her chance
sharing the ant and kangaroo's bed.

Her leg is covered by earth
that grounded her forebears first,
planted but free under piercing stars
fertile with the wisdom of dust.

(Lifesize red-tinted photograph in the Museum of
Western Australia, Perth)

CLAY

The river is a muscled snake
its blood thick yellow pureed clay
just off the boil under the sun's burner.

In the dark gold depths based on black ooze
river crabs live quiet lives until
hooked up they gleam dark blue

and transvest in the pot to red.
People and dogs stay on the surface
swim against the stream and float back down.

The hot current seems hardly wet
just not as dry as the crackling ground
and clattering eucalypts in the blistering breeze.

Outside the bounds of banks, expanse and distance
recall the taste of cool. On a far sandbank
twenty pelicans come to rest in a white design.

We need their feathers to withstand the clay
that coats our flesh, batters it for the sun
to fry and crust out the lie of softness.

We are not really soft, nor really white.
Black skin looks hard but it houses wisdom
free as riverflow despite our ravaging.

Bosnia

IN SARAJEVO

cold she lies on stones
dark hair winged
eyebrows perfect arcs
classic cheekbones.

The handsome man beside her
has turned away to sleep.
Their elegance
invites the camera.

Her wide eyes gleam
and you can almost hear
what she is telling
about her dream.

Her eyes are open
was there no time
or could no one bear
to close them?

CAVE WOMAN

Her home rubbled
she's gone back to the cave
to sleep with loosened hair.

The architecture of her face
its Modigliani clean lines
and straightened curves

houses eyes that see
beyond alarm clock
candle and newspaper

her children's faces
at tomorrow's assembly.
She prepares lessons

to teach them of
old tales of peace
far-off impossibilities

like safety and plenty
the absence of death
and the meaning of freedom.

In her brief sleep
she throws out a hand.
It meets rockwall.

A DOG'S LIFE IN BOSNIA

Our home mortgaged to fear,
when I looked at the coffee-pot,
the dog's scratch on doors,
they weren't real, we'd lost
the right to ourselves.

Enemies held the key.
The children asked and asked
and I had no answers, tried
to play games
and lost every round.

I begged him to leave.
I knew he should. But nights,
together I was alone but still
alive. They came, of course,
took him outside …

We couldn't move for hours,
days. Then I made food,
held on to the children, afraid
to look in their eyes. I still am.
When friends came to help

I went outside to find him.
Then understood why the dog
had not been hungry. How
can I live? Why do you ask me
questions? I have no answers.

STARI MOST*

Across a bend in the river
stood the bridge
white as the minarets -
rockets over the town's red roofs.

Five hundred years of spanning
proved strength and grace.
An exact shallow arch
whose sides buttressed town walls.

All a bridge should be:
a continual link
a crossing place
for ease and beauty
and a splitsecond shade
for swallows' throughswooping

built by Turkish invaders
who left it in the Ottoman retreat
to the original holders of the river

left a bridge and a faith to Mostar.
Both final targets for destroyers
in a most uncivil war.

*Old bridge

PLAYING FIELD

for Sean Bekric

That day it was football
a friendly for scratch teams
impromptu in a lull.
No league table, media coverage
just a few local boys looking on.

The mortars scored three goals
that knocked out more than turf.
After two Sean got up
went over to his friend
tried to pick up the pieces.

The third a header to his skull
called time for him.
He came round in a crammed hospital
eyes bandaged. Pain
broke all the rules he knew.

Broken bones block his nose
breath rasps and cracks dry lips.
He wishes they'd come
and take the darkness off.
Can't tell it it's night or day.

It was a field for war games,
the home side short on defence.
His friends left behind
their shreds and tatters to scarf
scored earth. His eyes hurt.

'I can see our family,' he says,
'our horse and cow and dog,
our farm's safe haven.
Clear as a picture. There.
Mother, don't you weep.'

QUEEN DRAGA'S KOLO
Belgrade 1901

They danced the kolo. Shuffled in a circle.
A closed circle that night. Soldiers all.
King and Queen went early to bed
read a French novel, slept.

By morning they were in shreds.
Bulleted and swordslashed.
Thrown from the window
to redden the green lawn.

A dance of death, really.
A clumsy attentat for no
noble cause. Jealousy.
That Balkan ease to kill.

ROCKS OF AGES

On the rock,
the Rock in the Sheep's Field
in Macedonia.
People enacted a rite
for over a thousand years.

To get a child, take a lamb.
Walk three times round the rock
then hand the kicking armful
to the knifeman above.
The lamb quietens,
gives its blood to death
for a new child's life.

There was a serious authority
here, as in a Bosnian field today
where a soldier slits a sheep's throat
and the gape of its opened flesh
shocks scarlet over the screen.
Fighting men must eat …

Birth comes with blood
within, without. Plenty.
Guns engender another
sort of sacrifice.

Meanings

MEANINGS

Say it in spondees, snow, drop,
two monosyllables
joined as a nursery word
you learned after language began

so it gradually lost two meanings,
became one, first flower of the year,
sent faint and sweet as air,
a kiss of life. Words meet

and change till the old pattern fades.
You suddenly hear the old meanings
of a frail yellow flower that has nothing
to do with a cow or a slip

far less than the drop of snow simile.
But a proper name capitalised
is a different part of speech,
the mineral stuff of naming

that rings like a glass when spoken
and calls up presence in absence,
the dent in a cushion, a footstep
or the echo of a voice.

METEMPSYCHOSIS

To transfer, transport or transmigrate,
carry across or over: no, that won't do
for something more like the certainty
felt at the moment of conception.
Yet that's not exactly it,

perhaps I've need of a longer word to cover
what Spenser felt about Chaucer, when
as he translated him, Chaucer's soul
moved in to live with his,
bringing its furniture.

It seems certain, but for us it's not
starting life or ending, not
one passing into another after death,
but a wholeness that leaves us both
free and apart together. Seamless.

KINDLING

Midafternoon dark and the drizzle
varnishes pennywort leaves
caches of green coinage on all walls

The seafog poultices tops of hills

Nothing remains of treeleaves but a piled gold rug
that won't wear long
sweet-scented with a brand called rot

You go down the path disbelieving light
apart from one gold windowpane
and the promise of flame in the tea-chest
scented with kindling
that the firemaker chopped before he left.

SHIFT

A sound behind makes you turn your head
as a dry leaf crackles to the ground -
not this time the murderer's tread.

Ahead round a bend in the path
a coatflap vanishes, leading on
from a timejerk into a hole in the past

where a tired man stumps home
to a supper of bacon, beans and ale,
the shelter of cob walls and stone.

Rags of crows grate in high trees,
a tawny owl terrorises mice,
woodsmoke thickens the breeze,

shrouds leaves and lives, time shifts
as your feet feel their way in old steps
that hold each, as the other lifts.

HABITUDE IN A CHANGED CLIMATE

The Ham is a dune cushion to lounge on
by the river's last swing to a mouth
that swallows the sea twice a day.

A new climate's hot unseason
baffles flowers and birds with winterspring
the sea changes tenor in confusion

Six cygnets are half duckling, half swan
two oystercatchers quip the silence, a heron
waits for a tide-change of food.

In the mist nothing much is clear
except the mud on our boots
and our long warm changeless habitude.

THERE

It’s not when you enter a room
and a voice sounds out of the air
by the window, in a suggestion of form
and a wind clears its throat on the stair.

It’s not the body-curved cushion or skinflake mote
a newspaper folded at the wrong page
a brown-scarred teacup, crumbs
that leave an imprint.

But the companion in the dream of hills
who walks with you into the bramble-fenced drive
and up to the wedged door that screams as you open
to an abyss or a catacomb almost alive,

who takes your hand and with an arm
round your shoulders, leads you away
to the garden where it is morning
and seasons as dependable as day.

PLANTING LIGHT

You plant anemone corms to bridge winter
deep enough to be out of mouse-reach.
They're grey to match the sky, hard pebbles
silently refusing the power of speech.

The dark creeps up behind your back, old leaves
hush and crackle, weeds hide under dusk,
night trawlers ride out with starboard red lights
and the house slides into night to a moon's disc.

Light lasts less and less. Between summer
and summer, dark's rule of tide
pushes and floods us, we switch to gold
bulbs, electric flowers, anemones inside.

ONLY ONCE

Clouds swim through the sky at the short day's end
salmongrey from the northwest
to spawn rain over the east.
Trees raise their branches, talk back at gusts
Waaaargh! I hear them in my hotbed of dreams
mixed with the sea's gasps. The rain's cycle,
months', years', circle our life as the woman's
who walked this path after similar rain,
boots clogged, sacking-backed, wondering
if her mother still lived or if she would see
her lie like the fallen trunk she has to climb over
as she has climbed over so much and only once
seen sun and moon rise at the same time.
as salmon and clouds too swim through the world once.

MIGRANTS

Before we arrived at the sea
a swallow looped over the road
a small wave making landfall
joyous after the crossing
billowing home to nest.

Alongshore the shingle shone
with an endless selection of stones
raven and kestrel cronked
and mewed near the quarry

and out over the silver-plated sea
two white birds flew westward
on a closely parallel course
as we walked east in the sun
hearing out on the skerries
the sad song of the reedbuoy
wingless and anchored
each sighing exhalation
the breath of its warning voice.

STREAMING DOWN TIME

Headlands shapeshift into whales
or the haunches of mammoths under the fog that feeds
in from the west. Rain shakes across
the clifftops, cloths of it cover
sightlines, rocks, contours and map.

We wallow along in it, catch at
possible signs. Ignore it as long as we can,
envy the nesting fulmars' resistance to wet,
ledged and secure, with all the answers
on wings or on eggs; we turn with the rain

to go inland off the hard ground
and on to the soil, walk necklaces
of churned butter-mud patted by tractor wheels.
Then swish over drizzle-steeped grass
that washes our boots, the dog's paws

so everything's fluid, polished by rains,
melted and blended, sharp edges washed clean.
Even our voices flow liquid
word after word down time
laved and streamed by the rivers of rain.

ABSURD

joy
in a featureless pub
with a dish
of flaccid sandwiches
and a pint and a half
of warm lager

But the food was on one dish
the beer pulled from one cask
and we sat at the same table

GIFT

you gave me a stone
unique
with particular history
I treasure it
though it is
hard
cool
and silent.

TALKING BOOTS

Four wellies stand close
in the back of the Landrover
while we sit apart
in learned converse
on the front seat.
Proceed step by step
along paths of reason
towards convergence.

THREE BEECHES

in three years will double their height,
forgotten the grip of pots,
free to spread roots in earth
and reach for the clouds. You'll plant them
after winter lacklight in a May
that opens out in silkgreen leaf
quickchanges into copper
deepens to bloodred.

In nine years they'll shade and shelter,
in 90 stand proud
over the garden breathing
and shining above your roof
shedding leaves in autumn
to free new points of bud,

when you and I
are a fleck on the wind
a glint in the air
a word or two that echoes
here and there.

A century more and they'll
fall or be felled
leaving their seedlife
to grapple and grow again
sign crown and bare branch
against the sky.

DAMSELS

Blue flowers
on stems of sedge
imprint green with cyan,
then move so each is a wedge,

a twig of life. It's June,
so why not plants that move?
Everything does. You, I.
I don't see a need to prove

wonders. But looking closer,
shortsighted, slow to spot,
like a cat, what's nose-nudging,
I see that flowers they're not

but demoiselles out for a lark
in the sun after a year
in amniotic muds. Getting
used to the lightness of air

they'll take to on reflet wings
thinking they're part of the sky
till a partner swooshes close
to play lover as they fly

head to tail and tail to head
in such a topsy-turved embrace
you'd think no life could come of it
till next year's flowering blues this space

STAYING POWER

that came with us into a village shop,
wings folded, with scarce a glance
made the counter lady cry
'Aren't you lucky? Aren't you lucky?'

and followed benign as we carried off
armfuls of nectar and delicacy:
sparkly cans and pork pies
to savour on the sea wall

and flew with fulmars alongside cliffs,
benign enough here not to aim
noisome nosy contempt at us.
Swooped in with swallows' landfall

and took our homage on that edge
that stayed uncrumbling under knees
so we could reach the word of rocks
spread open below. And showed us then

how seas sucked a crater out of a hill
down to shore level far from shore
caved in enormously - Round Hole
of yes or no, the start of breath

or lure of death. (Remember how
long snowcombers lined gold sand
and left signatures upon it
over and over in big scrawls

and how later we homed straight back
on our outgone tracks in all that space -
unerring route on a given way
here or there travelling always,

and scurvy grass blooms offered health,
two thrift heads flowered up at the sun,
and how at the end a kestrel swift
and fierce as time arrowed the sky?)

and still behind us driving, still
winged, stayed through difficult words,
stayed after parting, stays here
in writing and through time, and love.

EYE-OPENING

Clouds gallop from far to the west
in a black phalanx
as we snake up towards the tor
with a crawling column in tow,
coloured pins on sprung turf.
After a long sitting
in attendance on pain,
stiff with pity and duty, I look up
to see rags of rainbearers break into blue
big enough for a whole crew's trousers.

You open your hands to the sun
and I *see* again,
each flower of the bluebell field
a mile away over the valley,
at our feet a blood-coloured
tiny flesh-eating sundew plant in the bog,
in a given moment that cancels
all threat so there'll be no want
for *my* rest of what we call time.

While the wind that keeps giving itself
fills us with cold fruity wine,
twines in a gentle tornado.

LIGHT TOUCH

Long breakers draw in steady
as breaths to expire on the sand,
their whiteness gasps at sapphire,
their foam is light as a sigh,
though from above we feel
its muscle you must dive through
if you don't want to be dumped.

The visiting rock pipit's light
with a different weightlessness.
There's lightness and lightness.
The thing is to balance like birds,
accept rift or closeness
calm as ocean today, strong as waves,
brief as birds, light as a touch.

Hillson

HILLSON
A LIFE

{The finding of Hillson as a foundling, his house - whose ruins may still be seen - and his clock-making, are briefly mentioned in Willian Crossing, *Guide to Dartmoor.* I have imagined the details in this sequence.}

1. CLOUDBIRTH

The child opened his eyes
to clouds' mothering fleeces
against the glare of light.

Kinder than parent who left him
a foundling in a stone circle
of petrified dancers.

Delivered to the moor
and all weathers,
rain, sun, seasons,

to carry the weight
of time, stone,
flower, skull, world.

2. BROUGHT DOWN

A moorman saw ravens
circling down from clouds
grunting hunger,

above a wail
thinner than a lamb's
and alone.

He took the child
down to the farm
out of the high spaces

to the cradling
of four walls,
to fire's tamed element.

To the warmth of wool, milk
and hand's knowledge
of how to hold.

3. NAMING

They called him Hillson.

He gazed at the breathing circle,
suffered water and crossing finger,
the sound of a ritual
echoing
stone music.

Above a buzzard called
from a wheel of height.

4. TIME WATCH

'I shouted
to see and hear it,
riveted
by its white face
and pointed hands.

A half-hunter,
its face half-eclipsed by
a semicircle of gold
which protected it,
he told me.

Its heart
beat with the steadiness
of the man.

Most of all
I liked to see
when he opened it,
its wheels and works.'

5. HOME

After lessons
and evening milking
he was off up the lane
to the moor gate and the sky.
Made space
for his eyes
to range
away from the caged reek of farm.

Back to the company
of linnet, swallow,
buzzard and raven,
to stone row and circle,
massive dome of the cairn.

Wind through gorse and heather,
rivers and streams
talking down to the sea's
hiss at the edge of the land.

Clouds layered one on another,
he watched cumulus sail under cirrus,
changed and patterned
by contrary winds,
of blustering purple
before storm.

6. STARS

On November nights the moon
lit and shadowed hedge trees,
pillared the lane as he walked.
Stars littered the sky over the moor,
he shouted constellations,
hunted with Orion
rode Charles's Wain.

He understood time like Kepler,
measured it easy
as counting sheep or stars.

The sheepskulls he found
and ranged on shelves
confirmed the endurance of bone.

7. NEW CONSTELLATION

The farm sucked him,
gulped at his strength
with a mud-drooled mouth.
At night he fell
into a slurry of sleep,
book dropped.

Time was harder to measure
and talk was of war and when,
Napoleon's spies and invasion.
Southerly gales screeched
of armies and battle.

His skulls grinned. But his blood
heard other news,
as he walked the river
hooves struck stones.

Eyes exchanged eyes,
green for grey,
as she turned, rode the ford
and sliced the slope.
Suddenly, flowers flamed,
each oak leaf shone.

He could not believe
nothing had changed at the farm.

8. BEGINNING TO THE END

They'd walk
far into the moor,
further and higher,
through the summer,
speaking each other's words
for passion,
the same thought
in the same mind
time and again.

Her father, riding his boundary,
saw them.

Dark, stripped of himself,
he woke to a halved life.

She sent one letter, from London,
in a language he could not translate.

Her sight turned inward,
circled through absent seasons,
voids.

9. FOG

Fog on Stalldon Barrow
and northerlies slashing rain.
Then frost dropped ammil
to glaze each glassblade,
thorn and rowan twig.

He felt it coat fingers and toes,
thicken round legs and arms,
box in his heart.
He grew blinder than a slow worm.
Space shrank.

10. TURN TO HAND

The farm clock stopped in January.
He carried it down to Ivybridge,
outside on the coach to Plymouth.
Trudged through snowmudded streets,
noise and black walls.

At the clockmaker's
sounds changed. His ears
cleared, fog lifted.
He left echoing
with the tick of the smallest clock.

Charles Church struck six
as he started back, its chime
alive. The cold fell away
before him, into the dark
as he left streets for earth and grass.

11. TIME MOVES

In April after a pale night
before even birds woke,
on Stalldon cairn pain
quit with the dark.
He was ready to start,

watched the shadow
move around the longstone
as the sun travelled,
learned the age-old way
to measure time,

by shadow-reckoning,
before the craft of sundials.
Ignoring adages,
now he trained hand and eye
to turn and forge, solder, engrave.

12. THE EIGHT DAY CLOCK

Love had lived its season
but run out of time.
Craft was a steadiness
regular as mechanism.

Arrows: the second hand,
minute, hour. Wheels and cogs.
And then exact assembly.
He dared more, made his first
eight-day clock, an English lantern.

But the farm trapped him,
and loss persisted,
until the skill of his hands
helped him to make time.
The harvest of seven years.

13. THE CRAFT OF TIME

Craft mastered, life adjusted.
A workshop in the old cider pound
with lathe, throw, turns and wheel-cutter,

files and hammer, runners
ferrules and arbors, burnishers and chucks,
fitted to his hand.

When grief came he let it run,
turned from it to clock hours,
recorded each movement.

The clock journals stored his search
for design, parts assemblage
of works, hands and voice.

Echoes of their words
still drew him back
to river and moor

where cloud shadows
over contours
raced with winds.

Sometimes he stopped
tall as a standing stone
against the sky.

14. CIRCLE AND SQUARE

It could pull him back,
the place where he was found
cradled in stone. As he entered

the ring, sorrow let go, he'd stay
until light left and he slept
safer than in any ring of gold.

On the cairn he woke at sun-up,
felt the stones' hard pulse,
the push of magma.

This was the strong place,
the ground for building
and he had its measure.

Chose cairn stones
with a horologist's precision,
built foursquare

in the hollowed out centre
with a door to the south
and the view far down

over terraces
of slates and schists
to the sea's late blaze.

Below in the valley
the green path
led to morning.

15. THE RAIN GAUGE

'When I'd learned to measure hours
I turned to rain.
My tools could make a rain gauge,
a funnel in a vessel to catch
rainfall, and a jar
marked in inches proportionate
to the vessel. Then I brought time
to aid my testing, how much clouds let fall
in hours, in weeks. I had the gauge
outside my cairn-house
built on bones and imitations.
Thus I gauged time and rain.
As if I could hold either.
As if I could have
held her, my love. All
slips from my grasp.
Except that summer
when she and I were we -
were then and ever.
Needless to want more,
when one summer
gives full measure.'

16. TIME KEPT

If he turned from south and sea
and sat against the north wall
in afternoon sunlight,

he could look into the high moor,
slopes curving to slope
over and over again,

arms reaching for the river
that can never be held.
But tall stones marched

into his landscape,
and their permanence told
that what had seemed ruined

in a far past,
her beloved presence,
was his own.

Granite and thistledown,
his clocks, the sky and stars,
now as then, were there,

moving through all weathers,
times and seasons,
loss and gain.

A break in time

A BREAK IN TIME

I

We have set out slides,
projector and screen.
The group comes well-dined,
we welcome them to
views of shifting shorelines,
weight of ice and thaw,
traces of lives,
introduced with
your measured voice, my hands
changing pictures.

II

The headland noses out morning winds.
A waymark points south
to Brest, Guernsey, Ushant,
northward the moor scallops sky.
Charts, figures, explain a lot.
But not how eight
walkers come together.
A peregrine scythes over,
its pilgrim destination
no more, no less, mysterious.

III

We stopped here before,
planning the first walk,
at an old stone tower
built to spot enemy ships,
a finger of alarm seen
far across the high plateau.
We recalled codes,
flags, linking watch stations,
Now our guests read messages
signalling history.

IV

After a dayful of air
and space for cramped eyes
we circle a table's hub,
chairs spoked inwards.
Oiled with tea
four light voices,
four dark ones, run on,
Our closeness falls around them, its sun and rain
folding them in.

V

At the hotel
we map routes and lives,
cross-reference mutual friends.
The dining-room's scented,
sweet savours, delicate juices,
a whisky-laced coffee mousse
spice our tongues. Over velvet claret
you mix a well-matured Wodehouse,
I serve a feast of Blixen -
a piquant pair for dessert.

VI

Next morning we board
the ferry boat, thwart water
to scout a creekside.
Close-encountering binoculars
find waders sifting endless mud,
statued heron quick to stab,
kingfisher's jade-sapphire arrow.
We walk away from walls
into the mild savagery of landscape,
silvaticus, a whiff of wildwood.

VII

A clump of fungus in the hedge.
Elegant scalloped parasols
in graded sizes. White heads
look permanent,
marble or plaster.
We cancel out
their self-sufficiency
by this chance coming upon
that keeps them in dear life
partnered with us.

VIII

Eight for lunch outside the pub,
across the sunshined stream eight Aylesburys
quack suggestions for another round.
The drake casts a feather,
white curl, weightless hull.
It slides away, downstream but like
this map reference, your chart of words,
its image will stay
afloat as we set course
for near and far home ports.

IX

We've looked at schist and slate,
their weight of age;
and at the long gallery
of men and women walking here
linked to us by place and days
with time for being.
It's high tide when we say goodbye,
as the last guest kisses me
she closes the circle
roundly as last night's full moon.

X

We can't tell, in Giorgione's 'Tempest',
who are the figures in the landscape,
whether the soldier will go off to war,
the woman he left grieving.
Perhaps after this two-day break
our group won't meet again
but the views we've shown
of landscape's forms and our delight
are painted into us all,
hung in our times and tides.

I chuck their chins,
I've done it through more years
than they are given,
and with so much love.
They stroke me, slide me, glide
and pluck me tenderly,
caress me with a thousand touches.
I lift my voice, my heart, to them,
sing every colour of the gamut,
until the tree that bore me
sighs in every branch,
hums through each leaf,
shrieks in the wind.
Afterwards my songs
run their melodies in the dark.

Anne Born

Riddle from *The New Exeter Book of Riddles* edited by Kevin Crossley-Holland & Lawrence Sail (Enitharmon Press, 1999).

A Violin